DR. SHENIN SACHEDINA

MEDICAL EDUCATIONAL
PRODUCTS

D1314971

Hi! I'm Chemo Commando and this is my buddy **K.I.P.**

K.I.P.
stands for

KNOWLEDGE iS POWER

Along with my buddies
Radiation Rod and Good Cells
I'm going to help you
answer questions about
breast cancer.

All of us wish you and your family
luck in this battle against
breast cancer.

The term **mithu (me-tu)**
means "sweetie" for a boy,
and **mithulee (me-tu-lee)**
means "sweetie" for a girl.
This is in the Indian language
called Kutchi.
Metu and **Lee** were derived from
my desire to help the children
of the world when their mothers
are diagnosed with breast cancer.

Therefore, this book is dedicated
to the mithus and mithulees of the world.

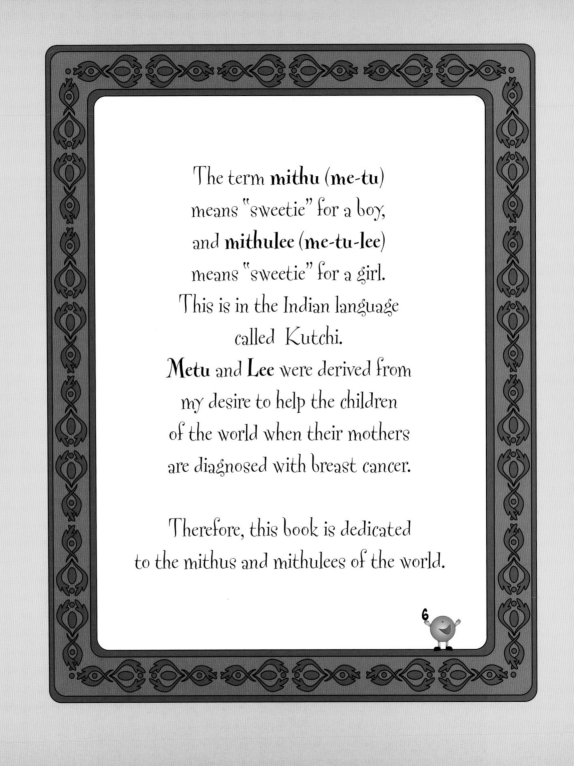

Hi! My name is Metu
and this is my sister, Lee.

This is baby Isabella.

Dr. Shenin Sachedina
BREAST SURGEON

It's nice to meet you all.
My name is Dr. Sachedina.
My friends call me Dr. S.

What do you have
in your hands, Metu?

It's my battle box. It has all sorts of toys.
Do you want to see them?

Metu and Lee, do you know why your mommy and daddy wanted me to meet you?

Mommy said you're her doctor and you're going to help her. She has breast cancer. We're not sure what that is.

Until then, Mommy can play dress-up.

She can wear wigs any color that she wants—even purple! Can you imagine Mommy with purple hair?

I'll tell you what, talk to your mommy. Maybe she will want to do both! You can do it, too. And how about Daddy, your sister, and even your grandparents?

Or do you think it should be blue?

Why is Mommy so tired all the time?
She throws up, too.

Mommy is throwing up because the powerful medicine in her veins is making her tummy a bit queasy. But it will happen for only a little while and then it will stop.

It sure is tiring fighting a battle with the bad guys!

Once the battle is done, all of Mommy's energy will come back. Then you'd better watch out, she'll chase you everywhere.

Who knows?
Maybe her super powers will make her even faster than you!

Mommy cries a lot.

You know how when you cry,
it is usually because you
are scared or hurt?

Mommy is crying
for the same reason.
Big people cry when they are
scared or hurt, too.

So you can do what
Mommy does for you.

K.I.P.

Making Mom
a card
is also a
great idea.

Give her hugs and kisses
to make her feel better.

XOXOX

20

30

Dr. Shenin Sachedina was born in Uganda, East Africa.

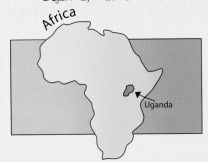

She immigrated to the United States in 1972.

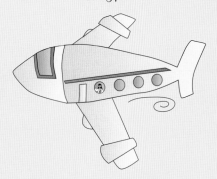

She is the founder of The Central Florida Breast Center in Winter Park, Florida, and has been in practice for ten years. She is a board-certified general surgeon, specializing in breast disease.

A Note from Dr. Sachedina

I am a mother of a six-year-old boy, Aman, and a four-year-old girl, Aznin. As fate would have it, my roles as physician and mother have merged to create *Metu and Lee Learn about Breast Cancer.*

This is the first in a series of books that will highlight different medical issues, with Metu, Lee, and Dr. S. as the central characters. It is my hope that this book, as well as all subsequent books, will help children understand different medical and life issues.

The subsequent books:

Metu and Lee Learn about Diabetes will focus on Sam, a young boy in Metu's class who has diabetes.

Metu and Lee Learn about Leukemia will focus on children diagnosed with leukemia. Metu and Lee will deal with their friend Chris who is battling leukemia.

I thank you for your support.

Best Wishes,

Dr. Shenin Sachedina

31

ACKNOWLEDGEMENTS

To my wonderful husband, Aziz— I love you heart and soul...forever, forever. I thank you for your help and support.

To my amazing children, Aman and Aznin—I love you both to the moon and the stars and the universe and back, and that's just to start with! Being your mother has been the greatest gift that God has given me. I thank God for you both.

KID A____

To my dad, the late Mr. Madatali Sachedina, and my mom, Roshan Sachedina— I thank you for your sacrifices that allowed me to become the person that I am. Every person that I help is helped because of your sacrifice.

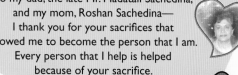

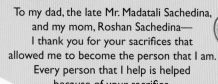

Michael & Sharon Winslow— words cannot express my gratitude. I thank you for your hard work and passion for this project

To my entire family, I love you with all my heart.

Karen Grindley—my right arm in this project from the beginning. Your passion and hard work were so greatly appreciated.

Tammy Sherman—whose talent and passion for this project made the characters in my head come to the pages of this book.

WWW.METUANDLEE.COM

Virginia Maxwell— thank you for being so patient in editing the text.

Marty Windsor— thank you for your contribution.

Aman Jasani—My six-year-old son for helping with the design of the characters and putting your imprint on this book.

Douglas Nesbitt— you're the man with a great eye and a big heart.

Anthony Clavizzao— thanks for your generosity and energy in publishing this text.

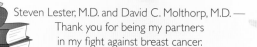

Steven Lester, M.D. and David C. Molthorp, M.D. — Thank you for being my partners in my fight against breast cancer.

www.metuandlee.com

DR. SHENIN SACHEDINA

MEDICAL EDUCATIONAL

PRODUCTS